Flowers of Perhaps

Flowers of Perhaps

Selected Poems of Ra'hel

Translations by Robert Friend

with Shimon Sandbank

Menard Press
1995

Flowers of Perhaps
Selected Poems of Ra'hel

1994 © translations: Robert Friend and Shimon Sandbank
All rights reserved

Cover design by Merlin James
Design, setting and camera ready copy by Lijna Minnet

Representation and distribution in UK:
Central Books (Troika),
99 Wallis Road,
Hackney Wick,
London E9 5LN
Tel: 0181-986 4854

Distribution in rest of the world apart from North America:
Central Books

Distribution in North America:
SPD Inc
1814 San Pablo Avenue
Berkeley,
CA 94702,
USA

ISBN: 1 874320 02 0

The Menard Press
8 The Oaks
Woodside Avenue
London N12 8AR
Tel: 0181-446 5571

Printed and bound in England by
Arc & Throstle Press
Todmorden, Lancashire

FOREWORD
by Yehuda Amichai

What may be most remarkable about the poetry of Ra'hel, a superb lyric poet, is that it has remained fresh in its simplicity and inspiration for more than seventy years. It appeals to readers of every kind — to old and young alike, and to those who are old-fashioned as well as to those who like to read the postmodernists. It has, in fact, become an integral part of what they feel and know, resounding in the ear and planted in the heart.

Until Robert Friend translated his selection of Ra'hel's poems, they had defied every attempt to render them in English. Now, because of his own ability as a poet and because of a temperament congenial with hers, his translations make it possible for readers of English to understand why Ra'hel is so highly esteemed. It well may be that her poems will eventually resound for them as meaningfully and memorably as they do for readers of the originals.

ACKNOWLEDGEMENTS AND DEDICATION

These translations are dedicated to Lois Bar-Yaakov.

The Menard Press and the translators acknowledge the assistance of the Institute for the Translation of Hebrew Literature, Israel. The translators acknowledge *Ariel* (Jerusalem), *Shirim* (Los Angeles) and *Modern Poetry in Translation* (London/Iowa City), where some of these translations and versions of the introduction first appeared.

The translators worked from *The Poems of Ra'hel*, Davar, Tel-Aviv, 1982. The 1985 illustrated edition, edited by Uri Milstein, carries the following copyright: © 1985, Uri Milstein and Zmora Bitan Publishers, Tel-Aviv. Our cover illustration is taken from this edition.

Robert Friend writes: "I am grateful to Dr Lois Bar-Yaakov of the Hebrew University, to Gabriel Levin, and to Reva Sharon whose comments and suggestions helped improve these translations and Introduction considerably. Carol Efrati and Jennie Tarabulus also proved helpful, not allowing any carelessness of wording, punctuation, or grammar to escape their vigilance. And I am grateful to Uri Milstein, editor of the invaluable book entitled (in English translation) *Ra'hel: To Her and About Her* and to Ilana Zuckerman who led me to it and provided me with many fascinating biographical details culled from it. Mr. Milstein's book includes, in addition to all of Ra'hel's poems, some of them written in Russian, information not available elsewhere, letters to her and from her, and reproductions of original manuscripts.

My especial thanks go out to Professor Shimon Sandbank of the Hebrew University without whose collaboration these translations would have been impossible. He provided me not only with a faithful literal rendering of the original poems, but with invaluable insights and interpretations as well. Sometimes he offered lines which I was glad to substitute for my own. He also contributed much of the biographical information I used in my Introduction."

TABLE OF CONTENTS Page

Foreword by Yehuda Amichai

Introduction by Robert Friend and Shimon Sandbank   1

Ra'hel's Book   7

"He too will soon go away..."	9
"Love was late in coming..."	10
"The messenger came in the night..."	11
"In my great loneliness..."	12
"Meeting, hardly meeting..."	13
Surrender	14
Pear Tree	15
In the Hospital	16
"Take in a clasp of brotherhood..."	17
I	18
His Wife	19
"Tiny joys..."	20
"Lay bare the wounds..."	21
"To see again those lines..."	22
"My strength grows less and less..."	23
Revolt	24
To my Country	25
Rachel	26
Transformation	27
Michal	28
Wrestling	29
My Book of Poems	30
"Was it only a dream..."	31
Flowers of Perhaps	32
Elijah	33

Sheep of the Poor	34
The Locked Garden	35
In the City	36
"You are not my kinsman..."	37
Barren	38
Jonathan	39
Metamorphoses	40
Visit	41
Our Garden	42
"I have recalled..."	43
From Mt. Nevo	44
"Pride commanded..."	45
"I have only known..."	46
"I have planted you in my garden..."	47
"I told all of myself..."	48
The Barn	49
At the Window	50
With My Own Hands	51
Recollections	52
Night Milking	53
Seedlings	54
Tenderness	55
"The fire of longing devours..."	56
To Shatter and Cry	57
My Dead	58
Notes (asterisks in text)	59

INTRODUCTION

Ra'hel Bluwstein, known by her pen name, Ra'hel, was born on September 20, 1890, in Saratov, a little town in northern Russia. Beginning her education in a Jewish elementary school, she went on to study in a Russian high school, where her courses included classes in sketching and painting, for which she showed great aptitude, and classes in Russian literature, which inspired her, at the age of 15, to write poetry.

In 1909 she came to Palestine as a tourist, intending to go on to visit Europe before she returned to her well-to-do home in Russia, but soon she changed her plans radically. Her tour of Palestine started out with a stay of several months in Rehovoth, then a small community, where some members of her family had settled. Here she gave herself up to a study of Hebrew, of the Bible especially. Rehovoth was followed by a visit, first, to the Arab town of Jaffa, which enchanted her; then to a number of settlements, where she was deeply impressed and moved by the settlers' dedication to their socialist Zionist ideals. Inspired by Chana Meisel, an instructor in agriculture, whom she had met in the settlement of Sajera, and who was to become a life-long friend and a powerful influence, she joined a small kibbutz – Kinnereth – on the shores of the Sea of Galilee. She chose this kibbutz principally because it had an agricultural school for young women. It was here she met A.D. Gordon, perhaps the philosopher of labour, and dedicated to him the first poem she wrote in Hebrew.

She had for some time been devoting herself to painting, less so to poetry, but she decided that in *Erez-Yisrael* her first priority must be working the land. Rather than practising drawing or music, she would say that one should "paint with the soil and play with the hoe". True to this new dedication, Ra'hel became one of the best workers of her kibbutz, which was remarkable in light of the fact that she came of an upper middle-class family, and that her life up to then had been an easy, even a luxurious one. Her father, although he had been compelled to serve in the Tsar's army for 25 years, had made a fortune in business. Her mother, highly cultured, presided over a salon, and Ra'hel's many brothers and sisters were all highly educated and some highly talented as well. A tall, aristocratic-looking and very beautiful woman, Ra'hel made a remarkable figure as she worked tirelessly in the fields. It was a hard life, the working hours were long, and the kibbutz offered only primitive facilities, but she was physically very strong and utterly dedicated. In later years she was to think of her years at this kibbutz as the happiest of her life.

She left Palestine in 1913 to study agriculture at Toulouse University, but on her way there she stopped for some months in Italy to study aquarelle. At Toulouse she continued her agricultural studies and managed to get her degree in spite of the Great War. But the war made it impossible for her to get back to Palestine, so she returned to Russia, where she taught children of Jewish refugees. It was a time of hard work and hunger, and she began to show the first signs of the TB that was eventually to kill her. Yearning for her beloved land, she was, in 1919, on the first post-war ship taking immigrants to *Erez-Yisrael*.*

On her return, she joined Degania A[leph], another kibbutz on the Sea of Galilee, but her stay there was short. Her now fully developed TB made her unfit for the life of the soil, and she was compelled to leave. Though she hated urban life, she went to live in Tel Aviv. Later she moved to Jerusalem, where she spent her last years in loneliness, and was often hospitalised.

She had many relationships with men, but never married. (She has even been described as the *femme fatale* of the second and third *aliyot*.)* One of the most important of these relationships has only recently come to light, with the discovery in a library of a batch of papers relating to her.* Among these papers are love letters written to her during 1915-1923 by a young Russian Jew, named Michael Berelstein. These letters reveal that their relationship had taken place during two of the years she lived in France, from 1913-

1915, and that they were still in touch long after they had separated. Together with the letters, the batch contained poems to Berelstein, written (significantly) in Russian.

She died on April 16 1931, at the age of 41, and was buried by the sea she celebrated. Her grave has become a place of pilgrimage where the "pilgrim" can find in a stone container next to her tombstone a book of her poems.

Ra'hel had only begun writing poetry seriously in her 29th year. Encouraged by *Davar*, and the writers who collected around that prestigious newspaper, she wrote articles and feuilletons for it as well. She soon had written enough poetry to produce several books, eventually collected in *The Poems of Ra'hel*, from which the poems in this selection have been translated.

The translation of her poetry involves a number of special problems. This is true, of course, of any poet. To create a translation, to find for an original poem an incarnation equivalent to it in diction and idiom, in tone, resonance and music, calls for a translator who is also a poet – one who, paradoxical as it may seem, achieves fidelity by being true to his or her own style. It cannot be emphasised too much that the result must be a true poem if it is to be of any use at all. A literal rendition in prose is far preferable to a poetic one that, although following for instance the original rhyme scheme, the original word order, does not come across as a poem in its own right.

Whatever the problems faced by the translator of Ra'hel, they are the problems presented by a very fine poet of beautiful (and deceptive) simplicity, and of a mastery of word and phrase that bring Housman strikingly to mind. That very simplicity and mastery make seemingly effortless and inevitable poetry (the ballad, the song) more difficult to translate than poetry of a more ambitious kind.

Like Housman's, her poems are limited in theme. "I have only known how to tell of myself", she wrote, but her limitations are more than compensated for by a depth of feeling that though powerful is always under control. She needed a great deal of control, since what Yeats says tellingly of Housman is also true of her: one step further and all had been marsh. But she rarely took that step, resisting the sentimentality that her themes opened her up to; for these dealt mainly with aspects of failed love, with her longing for happiness, and with her illness and poverty. Though the poems express rare moments of happiness, they mainly reflect despair, desperation, and nostalgia for those long ago days when she worked on the land.

Though Ra'hel can be described as old-fashioned, it must be remembered that she was also in some ways surprisingly modern. She was among the first to rebel against the pretentious, pompously heroic diction popular in her time, bringing to Hebrew verse a quite revolutionary freshness and modesty of language that relied for its effects on the colloquial. Quite in keeping with modern expectations is her preoccupation with "small" subjects. She is indeed strongest when she relies on closely observed detail, whether domestic or otherwise, i.e. "a cradle in a corner covered with white sheets", "tiny joys, joys like a lizard's tail", "the sick heart galloping like a horse", "the cow's warm breathing", and so on.

There are two characteristics of Ra'hel's poetry that raise difficulties for the translator: the regularity of her metres, and the occasional lapses in her use of a colloquial idiom. The translator's sensibility must overcome these difficulties in the interest of contemporary expectations. The particular musicality of Ra'hel's poems (many of them have been set to music and frequently sung) is often best rendered by taking discriminating liberties, by the substitution, say, of iambs for the anapaests that she, under the influence of Russian verse, especially Akhmatova's, relied on a good deal. Anapaests go far too trippingly in English. As regards rhyme (though rhyme is a staple of many of these translations), it is better not to rhyme at all than to stick zealously to a musical pattern that requires syntactic wrenching and imprecision of word or phrase.

The translator, too, must sometimes tone down what mars Ra'hel's otherwise simple diction, the resort to abstractions characteristic of the writing of her time — her over-use of such words as "happiness", "pain", "toil", "hope", "poverty" and the like, though their use cannot, of course, be avoided altogether. I found as well that the deletion and addition of words found in the original sometimes proved helpful. In my translation of "Jonathan", for example, where the original's last line reads "a little taste of honey" I have added the words "in the mouth" — an addition justified by the need to provide a rhyme at the very end which would allow the poem to end with a full sound instead of weakly trailing off. On the other hand, in "Take in a clasp of brotherhood...." it was deletion — the words "my dear and only one" at the end of line 5 in the original that helped, paradoxically, assure fidelity.

It should be pointed out that at the time Ra'hel was writing, predominantly in the twenties, Hebrew had become once more a language spoken in the streets. For millennia it had served mainly for the transmission of religious history, tradition, and law (the Bible, Mishna and Talmud). The language had been resuscitated in the late 19th century as a result of the Zionist movement and the re-establishment of Jewish life in Palestine beyond the small circles of ultra-religious settlement. But when it came to the expression of this now mainly secular life, writers found that they did not have a vocabulary adequate to their purposes. They were limited by the traditional literary language at their disposal and had not yet assimilated the colloquial, which itself took time to develop. It was Ra'hel, perhaps owing in part to her lack of a strong religious background, who took the first steps towards this accommodation. In this, she brilliantly succeeded.

Robert Friend, October 1994.

RA'HEL'S BOOK

By her grave her book
dangles from a chain,
as if the words had not
already flown,
and sown,
in hearts everywhere,
seeds of song.
Nurtured by despair
they flower there.

R.F.

"He too will soon go away..."

He too will soon go away
without a good-bye.
So his sad eyes say
and the bitterness that lingers
at the corners of his mouth.
Gravely he watches
children at their play,
or rages, and then grows suddenly still,
as if to say,
Nothing matters and nothing ever will.

We shall find him gone one night
from his place among his friends,
and suddenly pale with fright,
and a certainty of doom,
we shall all of us rush to his room.
He will not be there.
Only his last letter on a table,
staring blankly white.

"Love was late in coming..."

Love was late in coming, and coming
didn't dare call out: I am here,
while she knocked on the doors of the heart,
and stood as a poor man stands,
hands silently stretched out.
Her look was sad and imploring,
submissive and filled with doubt.

Pale are the candles, therefore,
that I have lit for her,
pale as the last of flowers
in the autumn light;
hesitant my joy, therefore,
quiet and in pain
like the pain of hope disappointed,
or waiting, waiting in vain.

"The messenger came in the night..."

The messenger came in the night
and sat on my bed,
his body all protruding bones,
the eye-holes deep in his head;

and I knew time's hands were dangling
(and though the words were unspoken)
that the bridge between future and past
had broken.

A bony fist now threatened,
and I heard aghast
sardonic laughter that said:
"This poem will be your last."

"In my great loneliness…"

In my great loneliness
of a wounded animal,
I lie for hours and hours. Lie silent.
Fate has harvested my vineyard, not even sparing
the young grapes.
But the humble heart has forgiven.

If these days are my last days,
I shall be quiet
lest my defiance sully
the peaceful blue of the sky,
my longtime friend.

"Meeting, hardly meeting..."

Meeting, hardly meeting, suffices:
one quick glance, fragments of obscure words,
and again waves of happiness and pain
sweep over everything and rage.

The dam of oblivion I built in my defence
is as if it had never been.
I kneel on the shore of the roaring sea
and drink my fill.

Surrender

He is breathing his last, my rebellion is dying —
that fiery, proud, and gay one.
Surrender, a pale widow,
approaches my house in silence.

She prises my clenched teeth open,
loosens my fists closed tightly.
She fetches ashes in handfuls
to cover the last of my embers;

and with head bowed down and silent
creeps into a distant corner.
I know too well she will never
leave my house again.

Pear Tree

Conspiracy of spring –
a man awakes and through the window sees
a pear tree blossoming,
and instantly the mountain weighing on his heart
dissolves and disappears.

O you will understand! Is there a grieving man
who can hold on stubbornly
to a single flower that withered
in a last year's autumn gale,
when spring consoles and with a smile
presents him with a giant wreath of flowers
at his very window?

In the Hospital

Hurrying, the white paths lead there.
A captive here, I cry
as I sit at the window gazing,
not knowing why.

"Are her eyes red from trying
to look beyond the hill?"
I smile and nod to the doctor,
and go on gazing still.

"Take in a clasp of brotherhood..."

Take in a clasp of brotherhood
my hand in your two good hands.
Both of us know that his wrecked ship
will never come safe to land.

Dry my tears with solacing words,
heal me of my pain.
Both of us know the prodigal son
will never come home again.

I

Quiet as lake water —
this is the way I am:
fond of children's eyes, daily tranquillities,
the poems of Francis Jammes.

Long ago my soul wore purple.
I wandered on the peaks,
one with the large winds
and eagles' shrieks.

Long ago. But that was long ago.
Times
change. And now —
this is the way I am.

His Wife

She turns and calls him by name
with the voice of every day.
How can I trust my voice
not to give me away?

In the street, in the full light of day
she walks by his side.
I in the dark of the night
must hide.

Bright and serene on her hand
is her ring of gold.
The iron fetters I wear
are stronger, seven fold.

"Tiny joys…"

Tiny joys, joys like a lizard's tail:
a sudden sea between two city buildings in the west,
windows glittering in the setting sun —
everything blessed!

Everything blessed.
A consoling music in everything,
in everything mysteries and hints —
and everything waiting for corals of beautiful words
to be strung by the imagination on its string.

"Lay bare the wounds..."

Lay bare the wounds of the soul and its pain,
exchange the gold coins of my secret unhappiness
for the penny of a pitying look?
No!

I'd rather with what remains of strength express
indifferent disdain,
and draw the line as always: Beyond this
you shall not go!

"To see again those lines..."

To see again those lines penned long ago,
the ink faded— how could its colour last? —
its wrinkled paper yellowed,
an odour of the past.

O memory's light touch,
O weight I cannot bear!
The sign is given, and the sign once given,
the distant is here.

"My strength grows less and less..."

My strength grows less and less.
Be good to me. Be good to me. Be
my narrow bridge across a sad abyss, across
the sadness of my days.
Be good to me, be good to me! – something of soul.
Be my heart's prop.
In the waste places be a shade-giving tree.
Be good to me!
The night is long, the dawn is far away.
Be a small light, be sudden joy,
be my daily bread!

Revolt

Like a bird in the *shochet's** palm you flutter in my hand,
insolent pride.
I stop your mouth,
I press together your wings,
and I laugh.
I've got you at last.
This is revenge for the flowers
 you plucked in their early bloom,
for your fences that narrowed my path,
for the world whose rainbow colours you made dim.
Lie down in your corner of darkness till I return,
till I return from him.

To my Country

I have not sung you, my country,
not brought glory to your name
with the great deeds of a hero
or the spoils a battle yields.
But on the shores of the Jordan
my hands have planted a tree,
and my feet have made a pathway
through your fields.

Modest are the gifts I bring you.
I know this, mother.
Modest, I know, the offerings
of your daughter:
Only an outburst of song
on a day when the light flares up,
only a silent tear
for your poverty.

Rachel

Rachel, Mother of mothers,
who shepherded Laban's sheep –
it is her blood that flows in my blood,
her voice that sings in me.

Therefore is my house narrow
and the city strange,
because her scarf once fluttered
in the desert wind.

Therefore do I make my way
unswervingly
because my feet remember
her path of then, of then.

Transformation

This feeble body, this sad heart
will turn one day
into myriad grains of fertile earth
waiting for the first fall rains
to burst forth in joy
towards the open sky.
I,

blessed by these showers,
shall twist my way
between coffin cracks and up
through saturated clods
into the wide day,
to stare at the khamsin*
with the eyes of grass and of flowers.

Michal

> *"And Michal Saul's daughter loved David—*
> *and she despised him in her heart."*

Michal, distant sister, time's thread has not been severed,
time's thorns in your sad vineyard have not prevailed.
Still in my ear I hear the tinkling of your gold anklet,
the stripes in your silk garment have not paled.

Often have I seen you standing by your small window,
pride and tenderness mingling in your eyes.
Like you I am sad, O Michal, distant sister,
and like you doomed to love a man whom I despise.

Wrestling

Alas! When the instinct rules,
my helpless hands are drawn
to the glamour of ruby and pearl,
to words as beautiful
as any precious stone.

They know its power is great.
What it plans they carry out.
It blinds with a shower of light,
makes deaf with a golden sound.

I cannot see the dawn
or hear the silences.
Was it I who swore faith to words
as simple as a shout?

My Book of Poems

My desperate cries of loss and pain,
of misery and rage,
have turned into a charming chain
of words on a white page,

sorrows of a kneeling heart
never told a friend,
secrets sealed in fire – exposed
to any casual hand.

"Was it only a dream..."

Was it only a dream? Was it I?
Was it I who long ago
rose with the dawn to till the fields
by the sweat of my brow?

Was it I who on long, sultry days
of harvesting
on a high wagon loaded with sheaves
would sing?

Was it I who bathed in the innocent blue
– under a peaceful sky –
of my Galilee, my own Galilee?
Was it all a dream? Was it I?

Flowers of Perhaps

Fresh flowers of perhaps once grew
in a landscape dewy and warm,
and I the best of gardeners knew
how to foster and keep them from harm.

Night after night, a sentinel
I kept watch tirelessly
to protect my buds from the cold wind,
the wind of certainty.

But finding out my secret, the wind
coldly outwitting me,
turned my garden of perhaps
into a cemetery.

Elijah

My room is like Elijah's, a high attic,
and sometimes there comes into my head
the thought of that miraculous old man –
how he revived the dead.

Seven times he stretched out on the child,
his prayer rending the skies; and then,
returning to the suffering mother said,
"Your son lives again."

Dear dead! – Not as before will Elijah come
to stretch out upon you with burning lips and eyes.
You are cold. No voice cries out. There is no one to listen.
And you will never rise.

Sheep of the Poor

My feeling for you
is like the sheep of the poor,
whose soft wool warms
a frozen heart, a tired heart,
a heart with much to endure.

My ewe is all I have.
I tremble with fear for her.
For what is the fate of the poor
but sorrow and despair?
I always knew that the rich
would take her from me in the end,
nor will they spare me now.

The Locked Garden

   to Z. R.

Who are you? Why does a hand outstretched
not touch a fellow hand?
Eyes meeting for a moment's space
drop in embarrassment.

Locked garden, and no path to it.
Locked garden, man.
Shall I depart? Or strike rock
till the blood run?

In the City

Although from day to day I grow accustomed
to this endless stone sea,
to the noise, the dirt, and the strangers,
I shall not complain or whisper: Galilee.

Only in the silence of night, in the sad hours,
in darkness without a star,
weeping I shall scrape with the shard of memories
a wound turning into a scar.

"You are not my kinsman…"

You are not my kinsman, yet so near,
you are not a stranger, yet so far.
Your tender touch evokes
embarrassed surprise.

Do you recall when walls closed in,
and we, over the throng of strangers, spun
from threads of our long looks
a bridge — a sign?

If you have hurt me, blessed be the hurt.
There is in that hurt transparent windows.
The path I take is not the common path.
My heart's at peace.

Barren

If only I had a child,
curly-haired and dark
to take by his small hand
as we slowly walked through the park.
A child.

Uri I'd call him,
a name clear and mild,
a fragment of light.
"Uri!"
I'd call him,
my small, dark child.

Still, like Rachel
the Mother, I mourn,
like Hannah pray
for the unborn,
and wait, still wait
for my child.

Jonathan

".... I did but taste a little honey .... and, lo, I must die."
   I Samuel, XV, 43.

Through the veil of distances, the sweet
face of a youth in splendid dress;
a constant heart in need: in the success
of battle and in retreat.

Jonathan, must you die? How sad the path
that each must follow in this world of strife,
paying with his life
for even a little taste of honey in the mouth.

Metamorphoses

Was I once a beast among other beasts
long before this life began,
and since have shared their sisterhood
and the fear of tyrant man?

Grey of feather, deprived of defence,
does a bird's soul flutter in me?
My melancholy song derives from her,
my love of liberty.

Was I perhaps a green blade of grass
in a life preceding those,
and therefore cling to my mother earth,
and find in her brown lap repose?

Visit*

In the evening, in autumn, in a worker's shack,
an earthen floor and cracks in thin walls of clay,
a cradle in a corner covered with white sheets,
and through a window distances leading away.

Oh honest toil and hope, guide me as you did then!
Oh patient poverty, that once I had!
The children drawing near grow silent when
they see the funny lady suddenly so sad.

Our Garden

   to Chana Meisel

Spring and early morning —
do you remember that spring, that day? —
our garden at the foot of Mount Carmel,
facing the blue of the bay?

You are standing under an olive,
and I, like a bird on a spray,
am perched on the silvery tree-top.
We are cutting black branches away.

From below your saw's rhythmic buzzing
reaches me in my tree,
and I rain down from above you
fragments of poetry.

Remember that morning, that gladness?
They were — and disappeared,
like the short spring of our country,
the short spring of our years.

"I have recalled…"

I have recalled,
more than once recalled
the sick heart galloping
like a startled horse:
everything in the light of a full moon
pale and unreal.

And in the silence, suddenly
a hint of fire
that reminds and brings tidings,
makes thirsty and satisfies,
wounds and heals.

From Mount Nevo*

The air listens.
And the heart.
Has he come? Will he come?
In every waiting for,
a never,
the sadness of Nevo.

Shore and shore
of a single stream
facing each other.
The stone decree:
apart
forever.

Stretch out a hand
in vain.
There!
No coming to.
A man and his Nevo
on a wide plain.

"Pride commanded..."

Pride commanded: with my own hands....

With my own hands
I broke the thread, I burnt the bridge,
and into the heart of an infant joy
I thrust the knife ...
                    with my own hands.

"I have only known..."

I have only known how to tell of myself.
My world is like the ant's, my pack
just as much a burden to me,
too heavy for my frail back.

My way, like hers to the top of the tree,
is a way of pain and struggle, mocked
by a contemptuous giant hand
and maliciously blocked.

All my paths twist, are wet with tears
because of my fears of a giant hand.
Distant beacons, you have deceived me.
Why did you beckon, miraculous land?

"I have planted you in my garden…"

I have planted you in my garden,
in my heart that cannot sleep.
Your boughs grow entangled in it.
and in it your roots strike deep.

There is no rest and no quiet
in my garden all day long.
It is you in it, you in it singing
amidst flutter of wing and song.

"I told all of myself..."

I told all of myself to the very end,
brought to the wine-press all my harvest of grapes,
and fell silent.
Will you hear my silence,
you who never heard my words?

The Barn

We used to sleep, you remember,
on top of a heap of wheat.
The shame when the first rays woke us
as they smiled through a pitchfork's teeth.

And as we slept, you remember,
all the streams of light
that watered the fields of the homeland
poured through us in the night.

And as they poured, they blessed us,
renewed us and fulfilled us.

That light is with me still.

At the Window

There is something after all of pleasure
in this sad world of ours:
in the small courtyard below, my neigbour's
garden of greens and flowers:

Two furrows of curling pea tendrils
aspiring towards the skies,
of onions over-cheeky
and radish with red eyes.

From the furrow below a figure
forgotten and loved in vain
climbs towards a high window
and peers silently through the pane.

With my own Hands

"Pride commmanded: with my own hands..."

I shall lock my heart's doors and cast
the key into the sea,
lest my heart leap towards you,
towards your voice far away.

And my mornings will then grow dark
and my evenings with sighs grow long,
my only comfort this:
my own hands did me this wrong.

Recollections

The old shepherd, Abu Tsalach, wakes me.
"Ra'hel, Ra'hel, get up."
The dream has lied. Like a ghost
down from the house I float.

The yard looks other, other,
and I am other as well —
tiny in night's enormous
world, alone and under a spell.

The sleepers go on sleeping
their sweet and dreamless sleep.
I share, initiate of the night,
the starry secrets it keeps.

Night Milking

In the yard – cold enchantments,
silence, terror of the moon.
Quick! to the shelter, the cow-shed,
the cow's warm breathing, and soon

my hands caress in silence
the huge horned head
of a life bound to my life
by a thousand mysterious threads.

Seedlings

In a garden bed I bend to see
a host of little soldiers,
brother seedlings of flower and tree,
of confident heart and stubborn shoulders.

With simple patience up they climb,
and climbing wound the battlefield;
and soon thin layers of earth
give way to them and yield.

O warrior-saints in the sad dark,
your humble courage shines
upon the weary and the poor –
a comfort and a sign.

Tenderness

How strange: those hard words of rebuke
were suddenly gone, those words of bitterness,
as if a miraculous wind had blown
into the whispering embers of tenderness.

No longer locked in that ageless, murderous
war between a woman and a man,
you became like a brother to me,
or a beloved son.

"The fire of longing devours..."

"The permitted there is and the forbidden."

The fire of longing devours
the strands of the forbidden
that I myself have braided.
Like flowers by the sun, I am drawn
by the mercies of tenderness.

My soul, hunched over the sorrow
of my life and death, stands bare.
O do not stare at me,
at the disgrace of my poverty.

To Shatter and Cry

To shatter and then cry over the shards,
that is my destiny —
no brother's hand stretched out to protect
that which is mine from me.

In vain at midnight I cry out
for a brother's hand to guide
as up my Mount of Olives I climb
with graves on either side.

My Dead

"Only the dead don't die."

Only they are left me, they are faithful still
whom death's sharpest knife can no longer kill.

At the turn of the highway, at the close of day
they silently surround me, they quietly go my way.

A true pact is ours, a tie time cannot dissever.
Only what I have lost is what I possess forever.

NOTES

p.2, l.23
The ship, the *Russlan*, was to become as famous in Zionist annals as the Mayflower in American history.

p.2, l.32
Waves of immigration during the years 1904-1914 and 1919-1923 respectively.

p.2, l.35
These papers, edited by Uri Milstein, were first published in 1987 in a book entitled (in English translation) *Ra'hel: To Her and About Her*.

p.24
shochet
a ritual slaughterer

p.27
khamsin
A hot dry desert wind, blowing through Egypt and Israel, experienced from time to time throughout the year.

p.41
The nostalgic visit is to Kibbutz Degania, the very first kibbutz, of which Ra'hel was a member until she had to leave because of ill-health.

p.44
In Ra'hel's Hebrew the word is "Nevo", not "Nebo" as transliterated in the King James' version of *The Old Testament*. The accent falls on the second syllable.

The poem. though clearly a love poem, is based on the following passage from Deutoronomy, XXXIV: "*And the Lord said unto (Moses), this is the land which I sware unto Abraham, unto Isaac, and unto Jacob... I have caused thee to see it with thine eyes, but thou shalt not go over thither.*"